IRIS
slow & t

by John McKenna & Sally McKenna

Time runs through the weave of Irish cookery, uniting those recipes that we call traditional with those recipes that we call contemporary.

• And time runs, again, through the weave of these traditional recipes, the time taken in braising, in roasting, in stewing, in baking. Making these dishes allows us to make time our own, pleasurable time spent stirring and tasting, time spent enjoying the cooking smells as they fill the kitchen, provoking our appetites for what is to come. Our aim is simple: to achieve deliciousness with each and every dish.

• There is a popular perception that traditional Irish cooking is limited in tastes and techniques. But, as these recipes show, that is simply not true. Ireland's fields, rivers and seas offer a cornucopia of fine produce, and we have taken that produce – rich butter, sweet beef, moist breads and cakes, sparkling fish, fine drinks of stout and whiskey – and tried to show how it can create ennobled, dignified, cultured cooking. Like every great European peasant food culture, Irish food is comfortingly delicious.

contents

bread

fadge

This potato cake also revels in the name 'titty farls', and fried in bacon fat, you will see why they are one of the enduring glories of the Ulster Fry. Kids will snap them up dusted with a sprinkle of sugar.

225g cooked mashed potato
salt
25g butter
50g plain flour
flour for dusting

With a fork, mash together the potato, salt, butter and the 50g flour. Flour a work surface, divide the dough into two halves, and roll out each half to approximately 1cm thick. Cut each piece into four pieces. Heat a frying pan until quite hot. Rub each piece of dough in a little of the flour on the work surface to give a fine coating of dry flour, and place into the pan to dry cook. Cook the fadge on a

irish food: slow & traditional

moderate to high heat for two to three minutes, and then turn when the side nearest the flame begins to brown. Cook for a further 10 minutes, constantly shaking the pan, and checking the wedges are not getting too brown. There should be a little steam from the pan, but not enough to burn the bread. Turn over after about seven minutes, and the fadge should puff up slightly. Cool on a wire rack, and when ready to eat the fadge, fry it in a little butter, or even put in a toaster and butter like toast.

bannocks or white soda farls

Bannock sandwiches are a treat. Split and toast a triangle and fill with bacon, sausage, onion and even a fried egg. 'Soda farls is fillin", is what they say in the North.

170g strong white flour
1/2 teaspoon salt
1/2 teaspoon bread soda
140ml buttermilk

bread

Place the flour and salt into a bowl and sift in the bread soda. Put a heavy griddle pan, or Le Creuset-style large heavy frying pan onto a low heat on top of the stove. Slowly add the buttermilk to the flour, pouring with one hand and kneading with the other. The mixture should gather together into a ball and come away from the sides of the bowl. Turn out onto a floured board and knead very lightly for a few seconds.

Then, using a combination of pressing and spinning, press the dough into a circle, approximately 1cm thick. Cut a cross into the circle, almost dividing it into four triangles. Lightly butter the, by now hot, frying pan with a little used butter paper, and place the circle of dough into the pan. Cook for approximately 20 minutes, turning after 10 minutes. Cool on a rack.

wheaten soda

170g self raising wholewheat flour
1/2 teaspoon salt
140ml buttermilk

Make the soda farl according to the white soda farl recipe, omitting the bread soda.

apple sodas

2 x recipe for white soda farls
1 apple
sprinkling of sugar

Peel and chop the apple and place in a small saucepan with a sprinkling of sugar and water. Heat until quite soft, but not mushy or falling apart. Make a double batch of white soda farls and divide into two balls. Use a rolling pin to flatten each ball into a circle less than 1cm thick. Place the cooled apple mixture on one of the circles, and place the other one on top. Cut the circle into four quarters and reseal each quarter so the apple is concealed. Bake as for the soda farl recipe — don't worry if the dough looks a little shaggy as it hits the pan, it rights itself during cooking. Cool on a rack.

bread

brown soda bread

Ireland's great bread. This is the one everyone packs in their suitcase when leaving, and dreams of when away from home. The secret of success is not to knead the dough.

350g wholemeal brown flour
150g strong white flour
1 heaped teaspoon bread soda
salt
1 fistful of wheatgerm
1 tablespoon kibbled wheat
1 egg
1 tablespoon black treacle
1 tablespoon olive oil
325ml buttermilk

Grease a medium-sized loaf tin. Mix together the two flours and sift in the bread soda. Add the salt, wheatgerm and kibbled wheat. Break the egg into a

bowl and whisk it with a fork, along with the treacle
and olive oil. Add the egg mixture to the buttermilk
and pour the liquid into the flour. Stir together with a
wooden spoon, until the mixture comes together. Do
not knead. Pour into the greased tin, coming right up
to the top of the tin. Bake in an oven preheated to
230°C for 20 minutes, and then turn the heat down to
180°C, and cook for a further 30 minutes.

white currant soda

'Spotted Dog' is the nickname for this rich, sweet
treat of soda bread.

400g strong white flour
1 heaped teaspoon bread soda
100g currants
salt
400ml buttermilk
1 egg
1 tablespoon honey

bread

Preheat your oven to 210°C. Put the flour into a large bowl, and sift in the bread soda. Stir in the currants and the salt. Measure out the buttermilk, and then beat the egg and honey into the jug holding the buttermilk, using a fork. Make a well in the centre of the flour and pour in the buttermilk mixture. Using a wooden spoon, stir everything together until you get a ball of dough in the middle of the bowl. Using a little more flour, bring the dough together lightly with your fingers and place the ball of dough onto a baking tray. Don't worry if it's still quite sticky. Cut a cross right through the dough, almost cutting it into four, and bake in the preheated oven for 40 minutes. Turn the oven down to 200°C and lightly cover with kitchen foil for the last 10 minutes of cooking.

buttermilk scones
WITH COUNTRY BUTTER & JAM

Look out for country butters such as West Cork's
Glenilen Dairy — and a good, fruity jam.

25g icing sugar
300g white flour
1 heaped teaspoon bread soda
30g butter, melted
300ml buttermilk
country butter & home-made fruit jam

Sift together the icing sugar, flour and bread soda.
Pour the melted butter into the buttermilk, and add to
the flour mixture, stirring constantly with a metal
spoon until the dough comes together. Turn out onto a
floured board and press into a circle 3cm thick. Cut
out circles, using an upturned glass. Place the circles
on a greased baking tray and bake in an oven,
preheated to 220°C, for 10 minutes.

bread

breakfast pancakes

These pancakes are like English drop scones, rather than the American idea of a pancake. In Ulster they are often stuffed with potato and apple. Eat with jam or honey, or savoury, with an Ulster Fry.

120g flour
salt
1 tablespoon sugar
1/4 teaspoon bread soda
1 egg
175ml buttermilk

Put the flour, salt and sugar into a bowl and sift in the bread soda. Make a well in the centre. Beat the egg into the jug of buttermilk and pour into the centre of the flour. Whip with a fork until the mixture turns to a smooth thick cream. Warm a heavy pan and smear it using some butter paper and a pastry brush. The pan should be hot but the butter must not smoke. Take

spoonfuls of the batter and drop them into the pan.
When one side browns, flip over, using a palate knife.
The pancakes should take 8-12 minutes to cook,
depending on the heat of your pan. This amount of
batter makes about seven pancakes.

Cool the pancakes on a rack. To serve heat them in a
toaster and butter. Serve with fruit jam or honey.
Otherwise, fry them in bacon fat and serve as part of
a fried breakfast.

ulster fry
WITH BREAKFAST BREADS

'Get the pan on!' is what Ulster travellers say on their
return to home, the promise of a bountiful fried
breakfast animating their appetites. The secret of the
Ulster Fry is really the specialist breads used: you
need potato farls, soda farls and pancakes to have
the genuine article, and you anoint them liberally with
sausages, rashers, eggs and puddings, and perhaps a
slice of vegetable roll, and lots of good hot tea.

bread

tea brack

Tea Brack is so called not because it is eaten for tea, but because the fruit is left to soak overnight in black tea. The bread is closely related to barmbrack, so called due to the *barm*, a yeast that makes it rise.

60g raisins
60g sultanas
black tea
125g butter
25g yeast
100ml milk
350g flour
2 tablespoons sugar
half teaspoon salt
1 egg, beaten
half teaspoon cinnamon
quarter teaspoon freshly grated nutmeg
40g candied peel

Oil to grease the loaf tins

bread

Soak the raisins and sultanas in the cold tea the night before you intend to make the loaf. In the morning drain the fruit, and throw away the tea. Melt the butter. Sprinkle the yeast into the milk and stir until it dissolves. The easiest way to make this bread is in an electric mixer, such as a Kenwood or a KitchenAid, and this recipe is given for one of these appliances. Place the flour in the mixer bowl, and add all the rest of the ingredients. Using the machine's kneader attachment, knead the dough for five minutes, until it all comes together in a ball, pulling away from the side of the bowl, and has a glossy sheen and a springy touch. Put a towel over the bowl, and leave the dough to rise for an hour. Knock down the dough and cut into two, using a knife. Place each ball of dough into a small greased loaf tin. Bake in an oven preheated to 200°C for 30 minutes.

Serve sliced and buttered. After a day or two, this is delicious when toasted.

bread

bacon & leek pot scone

This recipe was inspired by Herb Quigley, an American who once ran a country house in Tipperary with his wife, Chris. The Quigleys were fabulously imaginative bakers. This pot scone dates from the time when people would cook a loaf of soda in a covered pot over the fire. This recipe makes a grand sized loaf that is perfect to wrap in a cloth and take on a picnic.

700g strong white flour
2 teaspoons bread soda
2 teaspoons salt
600mls buttermilk

Filling
4 slices smoked bacon, cut into 1cm dice
1 sprig rosemary, finely chopped
3 tablespoons olive oil
1 cup thinly sliced leeks
2 teaspoons whole grain mustard

You will need a large casserole, or cast iron pot, or oven-proof saucepan with a tight fitting lid.

Generously butter the cooking pot.

To make the filling, sauté the bacon and the rosemary in the olive oil over a high heat until crisp. Remove the bacon and add the leeks, cooking in the bacon fat until soft. Return the bacon to the pan, stir in the mustard, and leave to cool.

Measure the flour into a large bowl, and sift in the bread soda. Add the salt. Then pour in the buttermilk. Stir, using a wooden spoon to bring the dough together, finishing off with your hands, perhaps with a little dusting of flour to bring the dough together.

Don't knead. Divide the dough into two. Press the first half into the casserole. Then cover with the bacon mixture. Press the second half into a circle to fit over the first half, and place on top of the bacon mixture, pressing the sides to seal.

Cover the dough with the lid and bake in an oven, preheated to 240°C, for 40 minutes. For the last five minutes of baking, take off the lid to brown the bread. Take out of the pot, and wrap in a tea towel.

soup

chicken soup
WITH POT BARLEY

Irish rusticity meets Jewish penicillin. This is a great
way of making use of left-overs from Sunday's roast
chicken.

the carcass of one roast chicken
1 carrot, cut in two pieces
1 stick celery, cut in two pieces
1 onion, cut in half
3 peppercorns
1 bay leaf
1 tablespoon olive oil
1 onion, finely chopped
3 carrots, finely sliced
2 leeks, finely sliced
1 cup pot barley
salt & pepper

Strip the chicken of any remaining meat, and reserve
for another use.

Place the carcass in the pot, and cover with 3 litres of water. (You can also add any left-over gravy or chicken juices, provided they haven't been thickened with flour or gravy browners.) Add the halved carrot, celery and onion, and the peppercorns and bay leaf. Bring to the boil, skim the surface, and simmer for one hour, partially covering the pot. After an hour, leave the pot to cool, then strain the broth, and, if there is a lot of fat once settled, remove this.

Heat the olive oil in deep saucepan and sweat the chopped onion until soft. Add the sliced carrot, and soften, then add the leeks and the barley. Stir, and then add the strained broth. Bring to the boil, simmer for 20 minutes. Season, and serve hot.

vegetable soup
WITH SHREDDED CABBAGE AND PARSLEY BUTTER

This technique of extracting maximum flavours from long-sweated vegetables was given to us by Carmel Somers, of Good Things Café in West Cork.

soup

3 large carrots
3 onions
1 head fennel
2 parsnips
a generous sprig of lovage or 2 stalks of celery
200g swede turnip
3 tablespoons olive oil
quarter of a green cabbage
parsley butter (see recipe on page 26, but including 1
   clove finely minced garlic)
salt

Chop all the vegetables into small dice. Heat the olive oil in a deep pan and add all the vegetables, except for the turnip and the cabbage. Add salt, and cook over medium heat in the olive oil to properly sweat the vegetables. Sweat for about 20 minutes to bring out the flavour. Add the turnip and cover with 2 litres of water. Simmer the soup for half an hour. Shred the cabbage and add to the soup. Cook for 5 minutes and serve, garnished with a coin of parsley butter. Add salt to taste.

carrot soup
WITH APPLE SODA CROÛTES

A sweet soup made even sweeter with the crispy contrast of apple soda croûtes.

500g carrots, finely chopped
3 onions, finely chopped
2 tablespoons olive oil, salt
1.25 litres chicken or vegetable stock
1 recipe of apple soda (see page 9)
butter

Sweat the carrots and onions in the olive oil and salt for approximately 20 minutes, until they produce a liquid. Add the stock, and cook for 30 minutes, or until the carrots are very soft. Purée the soup.
Slice the apple sodas into slices or strips, and toast. Serve the hot soup in wide, shallow bowls, garnished with a couple of slices of apple soda and a knob of butter.

fish & shellfish

smoked salmon
AND BOXTY

Boxty differs from potato cakes or latkes because the grated potato is not washed, and it's the resulting starchiness that holds the cake together. In parts of Cavan you can buy boiled boxty — a much more complicated but equally delicious mix of cooked and raw potatoes, but here is a simple recipe for what is known as boxty-in-the-pan. This makes a great brunch dish with Irish smoked wild or organic salmon.

3 large potatoes (approximately 550g)
50g butter, melted
1 teaspoon salt
pepper
oil for frying the boxty
Irish smoked salmon
parsley
sour cream or crème fraîche

fish & shellfish

Grate the potatoes (you can use a food processor to do this). Put the potatoes into a clean tea-towel and squeeze out as much moisture as you can. Place the potatoes in a bowl and season with salt and pepper and pour over the melted butter. Stir well to incorporate the butter. Heat a generous quantity of oil in a frying pan and place serving spoonfuls of the mixture onto the hot pan. Try to keep the spoonfuls the same size as this affects the overall presentation of the dish. Cook over a fairly high heat, turning after approximately five minutes. The outside of the boxty should be crispy, the inside just cooked. This makes enough for ten cakes.

To serve, place two boxty on a plate, and sandwich with a slice of smoked salmon. Dollop on a spoonful of sour cream or crème fraîche, and place a sprig of parsley or dill beside.

fish & shellfish

grilled lemon sole
WITH PARSLEY

Fresh fish is at its very best when treated with simple, appropriate respect. Lemon sole is popular, though critically under-rated, being the smaller sibling of what in Ireland is known as black sole, and in England as Dover sole.

Parsley butter
2 tablespoons finely chopped parsley
25g butter
zest of half a lemon
squeeze of lemon juice
salt (only if using unsalted butter)

fillets of lemon sole
extra butter
salt & pepper

To make the parsley butter, mix together the parsley, butter, lemon zest, lemon juice and salt, if using. The

best way to do this is to use a pestle and mortar.
Dry the fish with kitchen paper.
Butter a heat-proof dish and place the fillets skin side
down on it, and season lightly with salt and freshly
ground pepper. Place a generous teaspoon of parsley
butter on each fillet (you can either spread this out on
the fish, or leave in a dollop in the centre). Grill the
fillets under a pre-heated moderately hot grill until
cooked. Cooking time depends on the size of the
fillet, but the fish are cooked when they are white, and
firm to the touch.

scallops
PAN-FRIED IN BROWN BUTTER

A succulent and simple scallop dish, demonstrated to
us by Maureen Daly from Durrus in West Cork.
Traditionally, the plentiful scallops would have been
first boiled in their shells, then emptied out and given
this dousing in a hot, nutty butter.

fish & shellfish

For each 6 scallops use:
50g butter
salt and pepper

Dry the scallops with kitchen paper, and season with salt and pepper. Heat the butter in a pan until it just begins to foam (be careful, it will burn easily). Place the scallops into the hot butter, and cook for one minute. Turn over, and after another minute or so, shake the pan, making sure the scallops do not stick. The scallops are cooked after about two-and-a-half minutes. Keep the butter very hot, so that it coats the scallops with a brown glaze. Serve immediately with brown soda bread.

smoked cod pie
WITH CHEDDAR CRUST

We first saw the use of Cheddar to make a crust in action in the splendid Idaho Café in Cork city, where

fish & shellfish

they offer you smoked fish pies with a choice of
potato or cheese topping. Go for the cheese, is our
advice.

600g smoked cod
70g leeks
300g potatoes, peeled and cut into fine dice
handful of chopped parsley
425ml milk
175ml cream
1 teaspoon mustard powder
1 tablespoon soft butter mixed with 1 tablespoon
  white flour
Irish red Cheddar, grated

Place the fish, leeks, potatoes and parsley in a large
pan and cover with the milk and cream. Bring to the
boil (watching carefully, as it boils over easily) and
simmer for 15 minutes. Lift out the cod with a slotted
spoon and when cool enough flake the fish into bite-
size pieces. Strain the milk and cream. Place the
strained vegetables in a bowl with the fish, and stir

gently to combine. Put the liquid back on the heat and bring to the boil, stir in the butter and flour mixture, constantly stirring until the liquid thickens, and pour into the bowl with the fish. You can prepare the pies up to this point in advance of eating them. When ready to eat ladle the fish mixture into individual pie dishes. Cover with a very thick coating of grated cheddar. Place in an oven pre-heated to 200°C for 15-20 minutes, until the cheese is bubbling and beginning to brown at the edges. Serve directly from the pie dishes, with a green salad. This recipe makes enough for approximately six pies, depending on the size of your dishes.

oatmeal-fried mackerel
WITH BACON

This recipe is a fine example of Northern Irish cooking, where it probably migrated directly from Scotland, making for Ulster-Scots cuisine. We love it served with a glass of Curim ale from the Carlow Brewing Co.

fish & shellfish

For each person
salt and pepper
1 tablespoon medium oatmeal
1 mackerel, filleted
generous knob of butter
2 rashers of smoked bacon
lemon wedge
parsley

Put the salt and pepper and oatmeal onto a plate and press the mackerel fillets down on top. The oatmeal should stick to the fish. Melt a generous knob of butter in a frying pan and fry the bacon until just crisp. Remove the bacon, and keep warm. Place the fish, flesh side down in the bacon-buttery juices and cook for approximately 3 minutes. Turn over and cook for a further 3 minutes, or until the mackerel is cooked. Put the mackerel and bacon on the plate and drizzle over any pan juices that remain. Serve garnished with a lemon wedge and a sprinkling of parsley. Goes equally well with boiled potatoes or buttered slices of brown soda bread.

meat

boiled bacon and cabbage
WITH PARSLEY SAUCE

A collar of bacon from Gubbeen Farm in West Cork
will ensure delicious success with this archetypal Irish
dish.

450g collar bacon (rolled)
1 hearted spring cabbage (approx 1kg in weight),
* cleaned and cut into four quarters*
butter
grated nutmeg
salt and pepper

Poach the bacon over a low heat, in water to cover,
for 30 minutes. Five minutes towards the end of
cooking time, add the cabbage. Take out the cabbage
and chop roughly with a knife. Place back into a sauté
pan to warm with a knob of butter and some grated
nutmeg, salt and pepper. Keep warm over a very low
heat, while the bacon rests for 10 minutes.

Slice the bacon and serve with the chopped cabbage, parsley sauce and some boiled or steamed floury potatoes.

parsley sauce

500ml milk
half a small onion, peeled and roughly chopped
1 bay leaf
3 cloves
a little grated nutmeg
salt and white pepper
50g butter
20g plain white flour
large handful of parsley, chopped

Put the milk, onion, bay leaf, cloves, nutmeg, salt and pepper into a small saucepan and bring very slowly to the boil. Switch off the heat and allow to infuse for an hour. Strain into a jug. Melt the butter in a saucepan, and then stir in the flour. Turn up the heat and add the milk all at once, whisking as you do. Continue to whisk until thick, add the parsley and simmer for five minutes, stirring regularly. You can use the sauce straight away, but if you intend to leave it, then cover with a piece of butter paper to stop a skin forming.

roast chicken
WITH HERB STUFFING

Chicken and stuffing is the perfect Sunday dinner for children, of all ages. Use the juices and the crispy sticky bits in the roasting tin to make a speedy gravy.

Stuffing
50g butter
1 onion, finely chopped
1 tablespoon finely chopped rosemary and thyme
salt and pepper
100g breadcrumbs

1 free-range or organic roasting chicken
50g butter
salt and pepper

To make the stuffing: melt the butter and simmer the onions in the butter for about 20 minutes, until soft. Add the herbs and season. Stir in the breadcrumbs and allow to cool.

To roast the chicken: wash and dry the bird, season the cavity with salt and pepper. Put the stuffing into the cavity, but don't pack too tightly. Close up and knit together with toothpicks. Rub the butter on the surface of the chicken, and sprinkle with more salt and pepper. Roast in a tin in an oven preheated to 180°C for 20 minutes. Then turn up the heat to 200°C and roast for a further 30-45 minutes until the juices on the leg run clear when pierced. Leave to rest for 10 minutes, then spoon out the stuffing and carve the chicken.

meat

dublin coddle

The only dish that Ireland's capital city can claim as its own. Needless to say, controversy still rages about just exactly what you should include in coddle, but we take it as being an ode to good porky bacon and bangers. This recipe was given to us decades ago by Dublin chef Joe Kerrigan. We've never found another to beat it.

900g potatoes
450g onions
250g streaky bacon, thick cut
340g sausages
1 litre water

Cut half of the potatoes into 1cm cubes and the other half into large chunks. Quarter the onions and separate the layers. Chop the bacon into chunks, the sausages into thirds. Put water, onions, sausages, bacon and the small cubed potatoes into a large saucepan. Cover and bring to the boil. Remove any scum as soon as it forms. Then add the large chunks of potatoes and simmer uncovered until they are soft. By this time the small potatoes will have disintegrated to give a thick, soupy sauce. Serve garnished with parsley and triangles of fried bread.

braised steak
WITH TURNIP

This dish has a fudgy, savoury flavour that makes us think that, somewhere way back in time, *umami* must have been an old Gaelic word. Serve with sautéed potatoes.

1.5kg piece of braising beef, in one piece
300g carrots, peeled and chopped
2 onions, chopped
1 swede turnip, peeled and chopped
olive oil
a plate of seasoned flour
500ml beef stock

meat

Preheat oven to 180°C. Rub the beef all over in the seasoned flour. Heat the olive oil in an oven-proof pan, and colour the beef on all sides over the heat. Rub all the vegetables with the seasoned flour. Remove the beef, add a little more olive oil to the pan, and sauté the vegetables for a few minutes until coated in the oil, and beginning to soften. Place the beef back on top of the vegetables and pour over the beef stock to almost cover the meat. Place the pan in the oven and cook undisturbed for 3 hours.

When cooked the fat should have separated, the vegetables should be glazed, and the beef should fall apart.

beef
STEWED IN STOUT

Irish grass-fed beef and tart Irish stout were made for each other. Serve with boiled potatoes, which you should mash with your fork into the rich gravy.

600g cubed stewing beef (taken from the shin)
approx 25g flour, seasoned with salt and pepper
2 tablespoons olive oil
2 onions, finely chopped
3 large carrots, cut into 1cm discs
1 bay leaf
330ml stout
150g prunes
bunch parsley, finely chopped

Toss the beef in the seasoned flour and sauté in one tablespoon of the olive oil. Remove when brown and add 1 further tablespoon of the oil. Toss the onion in what remains of the flour, and soften in the hot oil. Add the carrots and bay leaf. Return the beef to the pan, and then pour over the stout, scraping from the bottom of the pan. Cover tightly, and simmer on top of the stove for 1¹/₂ hours.

Add the prunes and the parsley, and simmer for a further 30 minutes. The stew is now ready, but would benefit from being left overnight. This mellows any bitterness left in the stout gravy.

meat

spiced beef
TWO WAYS

Spiced beef is the great beef speciality of Cork city,
where the pimento-spiced meat is sold all year long.
Elsewhere, it is prepared by butchers especially for
Christmas.

1 large piece of spiced beef (available in butchers,
* especially around Christmas)*
1 bottle stout (for boiled beef)
1 carrot, roughly chopped
1 stick celery, roughly chopped
1 onion, roughly chopped

Wash the beef to remove some of the spices and
then, for boiled beef, place in a pot and pour over a
bottle of stout, and then add water to cover. Add the
carrot, celery and onion and bring to the boil. Simmer
for 30 minutes for every 500g of beef.
Or, for braised spiced beef, put the beef in an oven-

proof pan on top of the sliced carrot, celery and
onion, and pour over 50ml of stout for every 500g of
beef. Cover the pot tightly with a layer of silver foil
and a tight-fitting lid and bake in an oven preheated to
180°C for 30 minutes per 500g.

For smaller cuts of beef, (with both methods) add an
extra 20 minutes cooking time to the core 30 minutes
to ensure the beef is cooked.

Serve sliced with parsley sauce (see recipe on page
33) and boiled potatoes. Then use the left-overs with
an avocado salad which, although avocados are not
native to Ireland, has become a contemporary
accompaniment to cold spiced beef.

fillet of pork
WITH A WHISKEY SAUCE

The fillet of pork is a favourite cut in Ireland, and
should be cooked quickly, because it has no fat to
stop it from drying out. Whiskey has long been a
favoured ingredient medicinally, culinarily and socially.

meat

1 fillet of pork
salt and pepper
20g butter
1 tablespoon oil
3 cloves
2 capfuls (ie 50mls) whiskey
80ml cream

Wash and dry the pork and cut into medallions, 2.5-3cm thick. Season with salt and pepper. Heat the butter and oil in a pan until bubbling hot. Add the meat and cloves. Agitate the meat for a few seconds to make sure it does not stick. Cook over a steady, hot heat for five minutes. Turn over and cook for another five minutes, at which time the pork should begin to release its juices. Turn up the heat. Add the whiskey, burn off the alcohol and then turn the heat down a little and add the cream. Stir together. Replace the lid on the pan, turn off the heat and leave to rest for 5 minutes. Taste and season, and then serve.

leg of lamb
WITH ROSEMARY GRAVY

Irish lamb has a sweet, herby richness, perfectly revealed by roasting with aromatic rosemary.

1 small leg of lamb
3 generous sprigs of fresh rosemary
50g butter
salt and pepper
1 carrot, sliced lengthways into four
1 onion, cut in quarters
2 stalks of celery, halved lengthways
2 cloves garlic, peeled and bruised with the handle of
*   a knife*
350ml potato water, vegetable or lamb stock, or water

Heat the oven to 230°C. Chop one of the sprigs of rosemary, and mix with the butter, salt and pepper. Smear over the lamb. Place the carrot, onion, celery, garlic and the remaining rosemary on a shallow baking tray and place the lamb on top. Roast for 20 minutes in the hot oven, then turn down the oven and roast for 40 to 60 minutes more, depending on how well cooked you like your meat.

Remove the meat and keep covered to rest while you make the gravy. Place the baking tray on the hob and pour in the stock or water. Scrape the pan to get all the caramelised bits at the bottom. Then strain the whole lot into a small saucepan, pressing the vegetables, particularly the carrot and the garlic through the sieve. Don't be tempted to thicken the gravy; this is a lovely, light, rosemary-scented jus. Carve the lamb, and serve with the gravy and a sprig of fresh rosemary. The meat goes sublimely well with green vegetables and roast potatoes.

irish stew

Irish Stew is not just the standard bearer of Irish cooking, it is actually the mother of all European

daubes and braises. For us, it remains the supreme
example of all such inventions: the original and the
best.

900g neck of lamb chops
900g potatoes, thickly sliced
350g onions, thinly sliced
salt and pepper
1 handful mixed herbs (rosemary, thyme, parsley), very
* finely chopped*
water

You will need a very large casserole dish, into which
you layer the ingredients in the following order:
potatoes, onions, lamb, potatoes, onions, lamb, and
finishing with a layer of potatoes. Season with the salt,
pepper and herbs after each layer of potatoes. Pour
over water, almost to cover. Bake in the oven,
preheated to 180°C, for three hours.

parsnip and carrot mash

A sweet'n'lovely mixture that is one of the archetypes of Irish vegetable cookery.

550g parsnips
350g carrots
salt, pepper and freshly grated nutmeg
1 tablespoon butter

Peel the parsnips and cut out their woody cores by splitting them in half lengthways, then in half again, and cutting out the woody centre. Peel the carrots. Dice all the vegetables to a uniform small dice. Place the carrots into a medium-sized saucepan and almost cover with water. Bring to the boil, and after five or six minutes add the parsnips. Cook all the vegetables until soft. Drain, season with salt, pepper and nutmeg, and then crush, using a potato masher, until the orange and white are well mixed, but not smooth. Beat in a tablespoon of butter with a fork, and serve.

champ

The ideal champ should be nutty from a little reduced cream – a little trick we learned from Simon McCance of the Yellow Door in Northern Ireland – and fresh from the raw greenness of the spring onions, which do their bit to cut the richness of the dish. When properly cooked, champ is one of Ireland's greatest potato dishes.

1kg main crop floury potatoes
1 bunch scallions (spring onions), approximately 100g,
* white and green parts*
100ml cream
50g butter
ssalt and pepper

Peel and wash the potatoes. Cut into large dice and put in a medium saucepan, and just cover with water. Simmer, partially covered, until soft. There should be no 'give' in the potato when pierced with a knife. Meanwhile trim the scallions, keeping as much of the green as you can, and thinly slice on the diagonal. Pour the cream into a small saucepan and boil to reduce by half. When the potatoes are cooked, pour off the water. Leave the lid ajar and let the cooked potatoes rest and dry over a low heat, when they will become floury. Mash the potatoes using a potato masher. Season the potatoes with salt and pepper, and then, with a fork, whip in the cream, the butter and finally the scallions. Serve with a little — or a lot — more butter on top.

colcannon

A great winter dish of potatoes and cabbage, and also a great dish for a party: tradition has it that if you secrete a ring in the bowl of colcannon, let everyone eat away at it with spoons, then whoever finds the ring will be next to marry. The Irish can find an excuse for matchmaking almost anywhere.

750g potatoes
1 small onion, finely chopped
50g butter
350g cabbage, shredded
nutmeg
salt and pepper
parsley
milk
butter for serving

Cook the potatoes in water to cover. Soften the onion in the butter, and add the shredded cabbage, the nutmeg, salt and pepper. Cook until the cabbage is soft. Mash the cooked potatoes and then stir in the onion and cabbage mixture. Add some finely chopped parsley and a little milk if the mixture is dry. Whip up with a fork, and serve with some more butter.

sweet things

free-range egg sponge
WITH GERANIUM JELLY

The idea for this recipe came from Jim Tynan in The Kitchen in Portlaoise, who in turn was inspired by the Geranium Jellies made by Rosarie O'Byrne of the West Cork Herb Farm.

4 large free-range eggs
110g caster sugar
110g flour, sifted
170ml cream
a punnet of fresh strawberries, sliced
geranium jelly
icing sugar to dust

Preheat the oven to 180°C. Grease two small sandwich tins. Separate the eggs and beat the yolks with the sugar until they reach the ribbon stage, ie the whisk leaves a mark in the mix. Whisk the whites until they form stiff peaks. Fold the yolks into the flour using a metal spoon, and then gently fold in the whites, trying not to lose the air generated in the beating. Divide the mixture between the two tins, and bake in an oven preheated to 180ºC for 20 minutes. Leave to cool, at which point they will come away from the side of the tins. Place one sponge on a serving plate and spread with plenty of geranium jelly (we've made this successfully with rose petal jelly as well). Whip the cream, spread on top of the jelly, and dot on some strawberries. Place the second sponge on top, dust with icing sugar, and if you like, decorate with a few more slices of strawberry.

butterfly cakes
WITH APPLE BUTTER ICING

These little sponge cakes are as light and ethereal as a butterfly's wings. Thanks to Lelia McKenna for the recipe.

sweet things

100g self-raising white flour
1 teaspoon baking powder
100g baking margarine
100g caster sugar
2 free-range eggs

Apple Purée
2 dessert apples
20ml water
30g caster sugar
squeeze of lemon

Butter Icing
50g butter
30g icing sugar
drop of milk

icing sugar for dusting

Preheat oven to 180°C. To make the cakes: Sift the
flour and baking powder. Mix together the margarine
and sugar, beating with a wooden spoon to combine.
Beat the eggs. Pour the egg mixture into the butter

and sugar, and beat to fully combine. Stir in the flour mixture. Pour into 12 little paper cases and bake in an oven preheated to 180°C for 15 minutes.

Meanwhile make the two icings. Peel, core and roughly chop the apples. Put them together with the water, sugar and lemon into a small pan, and heat until very soft. Buzz gun to a very smooth consistency. Make the butter icing by beating the butter and sugar with a drop of milk, using electric beaters.

When the cakes are cooked and cooled, take a teaspoon and describe a circle in the top of each cake, cutting out a chunk of sponge. Fill the cakes with the two toppings. Cut the removed chunk into two pieces, and place on top of the toppings, like two butterfly wings. Sprinkle the whole lot with icing sugar just before serving.

sweet things

rhubarb crumble

There isn't a person alive who doesn't love crumble
and, made with tart rhubarb, it is a masterly pudding.

100g white flour
50g dark brown sugar
20g granulated sugar
100g butter
500g rhubarb
2 tablespoons flour, mixed with 2 tablespoons sugar

Mix together the white flour, dark brown sugar and
granulated sugar. Break the butter into pieces, and,
with your fingers, crumble it into the flour and sugar
mix until you get a crumble. Cut the rhubarb into
medium-sized pieces and toss in the flour and sugar.
Place in a shallow ovenproof dish and top with the
crumble. Bake in an oven, preheated to 200°C, for 35
minutes. Serve hot, with Irish artisan ice cream.

buttermilk smoothie

People always used to drink buttermilk in Ireland, and when you taste a hand-made, artisan buttermilk you will understand why. In our more industrial world, the buttermilk stands being jazzed up into a delicious, tart smoothie.

4 strawberries
2 tablespoons natural yogurt
half cup buttermilk
1 cup of fresh apple juice, or apple and raspberry juice

Combine all the ingredients together in a blender and whizz. This makes enough for two refreshing glasses.

Bord Bía
Irish Food Board

Ireland's speciality food and drink sector is internationally renowned. Bord Bia recognises that this sector has been built upon two important elements: a fertile landscape covered predominantly by well-watered grass that provides perfect growing conditions for both livestock and crops, and highly skilled producers who possess a unique understanding of and respect for the goodness this land produces.

• Family-run businesses and small companies craft natural ingredients into a diverse range of food and drink products. Many use recipes handed down through the generations, while others add new influences from further afield. Products available range from farmhouse cheeses and traditional soda breads, through to naturally brewed ales and newer products such as herb-infused oils and live yoghurts. In all cases the care and creativity that producers apply to their craft come shining through in the uniquely Irish flavours of the food and drink produced.

• Britain and Ireland continues to be the core geographic markets for the sector although certain categories such as farmhouse cheeses sell in over 25 geographic territories worldwide. The USA is a growth market for Irish farmhouse cheese and more recently France, Australia and Japan are emerging markets for the category.

• Bord Bia's Small Business programme centres around key areas of trade marketing to identify emerging opportunities, securing new listings and

bord bia

sustaining existing business. Bord Bia works with industry bodies such as CAIS, Eurotoques and the recently established Taste Council.

• The TASTE Council, co-ordinated by Bord Bia, continues to build awareness for the speciality and artisan sector and has made a number of policy submissions to government committees about the role and importance of the sector.

• Bord Bia, in conjunction with Slow Food, will sponsor the first university of gastronomic science in Italy. The curriculum will include a programme on science, history, culture and gastronomy of Irish food and participants will be from all over the world. Slow Food is a growing consumer food movement with over 100,000 members.

Background information

**ASSOCIATIONS & INDIVIDUALS WORKING IN
IRISH FOOD**
**Find out more about Ireland's food culture and
speciality producers by visiting the following
websites:**

- **Bord Bia, the Irish Food Board**
www.bordbia.ie
www.bordbia.ie/Consumers/Buying_Food/Buy_Direct

- **Ireland's Farmers' Markets**
www.irelandmarkets.com

- **Ireland's Artisan Cheesemakers**
www.irishcheese.ie

- **Organic Growers' Associations in Ireland**
www.irishorganic.ie
http://www.iol.ie/~organic/

directory

• **Slow Food in Ireland**
www.slowfoodireland.com

• **information on Northern Ireland**
www.foodstuffireland.com
www.investni.com

• **Irish speciality food portal**
www.bridgestoneguides.com

• **Irish seafood producers**
www.iasc.ie

• **speciality butchers in Ireland**
www.craftbutchers.ie

• **Artisan, guild of bakers, Northern Ireland**
www.dittysbakery.com

TRADITIONAL FOODS
**Some traditional artisan foods mentioned in the
book can be sourced from the following
addresses:**

directory

• artisan dairy products
Glenilen Farm, www.glenilen.com
Knockatee Organic Dairy knockateedairy@eircom.net
West Cork Natural Cheese, Schull, Co Cork
Artisan cheesemakers addresses can be found by
visiting www.irishcheese.ie

• bacon and ham
www.blackbacon.com
www.caherbegfreerangepork.ie
www.gubbeen.com
www.moyallonfoods.com
www.thepinkpig.com

• craft breweries
www.beb.ie
www.carlowbrewing.com
www.dublinbrewing.com
www.dublinpubs.com
www.kinsalebrewing.com

directory

• smoked products
www.burrensmokehouse.ie
www.drumgoolandsmokehouse.co.uk
www.dunns.ie
www.frankhederman.com
www.kinvarasmokedsalmon.com
www.smokehouse.ie
www.ummera.com

• specialist retailers
www.countrychoice.ie
www.koconnellsfish.com
www.sheridanscheesemongers.com
www.urru.ie

• cookery schools
www.ballyknocken.com
www.cookingisfun.ie
www.irishcookeryschool.com
www.thegoodthingscafe.com

irish food: slow & traditional

index

index

irish food: slow & traditional